FINGERPICKING
ACOUSTIC HITS

Music arrangements by Chad Johnson

ISBN 978-1-4950-6426-5

HAL•LEONARD®

7777 W. BLUEMOUND RD. P.O. BOX 13819 MILWAUKEE, WI 53213

Visit Hal Leonard Online at
www.halleonard.com

INTRODUCTION TO FINGERSTYLE GUITAR

Fingerstyle (a.k.a. fingerpicking) is a guitar technique that means you literally pick the strings with your right-hand fingers and thumb. This contrasts with the conventional technique of strumming and playing single notes with a pick (a.k.a. flatpicking). For fingerpicking, you can use any type of guitar: acoustic steel-string, nylon-string classical, or electric.

THE RIGHT HAND

The most common right-hand position is shown here.

Use a high wrist; arch your palm as if you were holding a ping-pong ball. Keep the thumb outside and away from the fingers, and let the fingers do the work rather than lifting your whole hand.

The thumb generally plucks the bottom strings with downstrokes on the left side of the thumb and thumbnail. The other fingers pluck the higher strings using upstrokes with the fleshy tip of the fingers and fingernails. The thumb and fingers should pluck one string per stroke and not brush over several strings.

Another picking option you may choose to use is called hybrid picking (a.k.a. plectrum-style fingerpicking). Here, the pick is usually held between the thumb and first finger, and the three remaining fingers are assigned to pluck the higher strings.

THE LEFT HAND

The left-hand fingers are numbered 1 through 4.

Be sure to keep your fingers arched, with each joint bent; if they flatten out across the strings, they will deaden the sound when you fingerpick. As a general rule, let the strings ring as long as possible when playing fingerstyle.

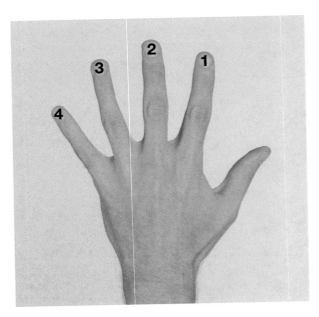

The A Team

Words and Music by Ed Sheeran

*T=Thumb on 6th string

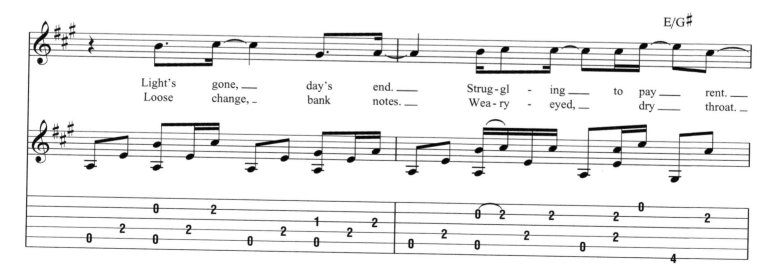

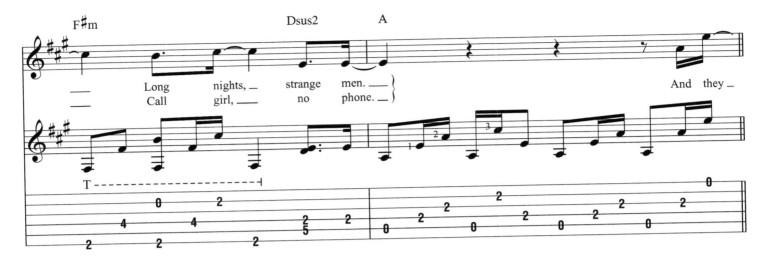

Long nights, __ strange men. __
Call girl, __ no phone.

And they __

Chorus

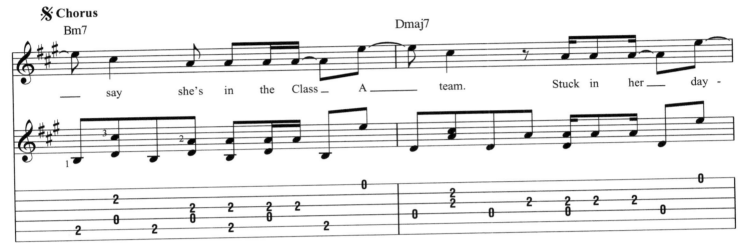

__ say she's in the Class __ A __ team. Stuck in her __ day -

- dream. Been this way __ since eight - een, __ but late - ly __ her

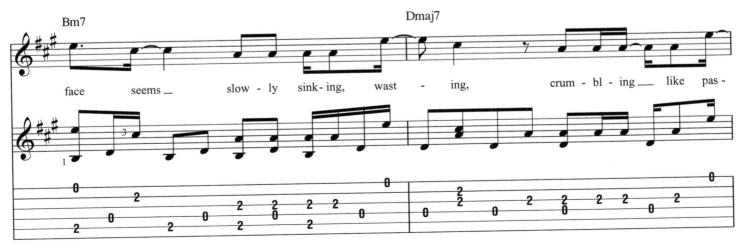

face seems __ slow - ly sink - ing, wast - ing, crum - bl - ing __ like pas -

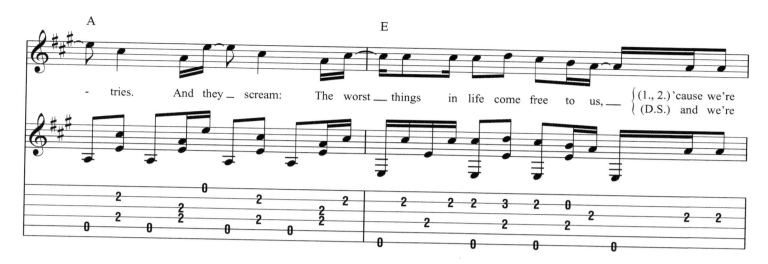

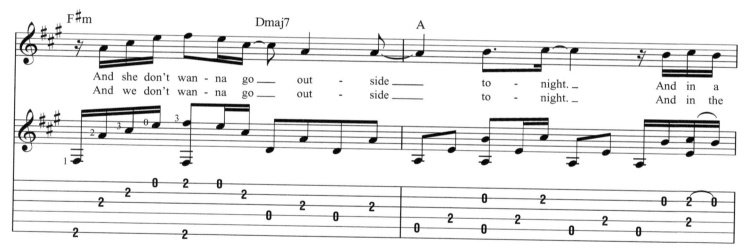

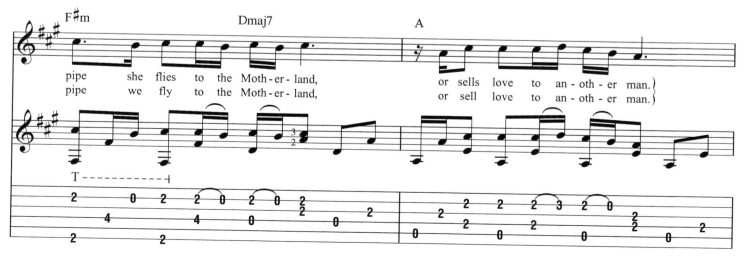

It's too cold _____ out - side _____ for an - gels to fly. __

1.

For an - gels to fly. __

To Coda

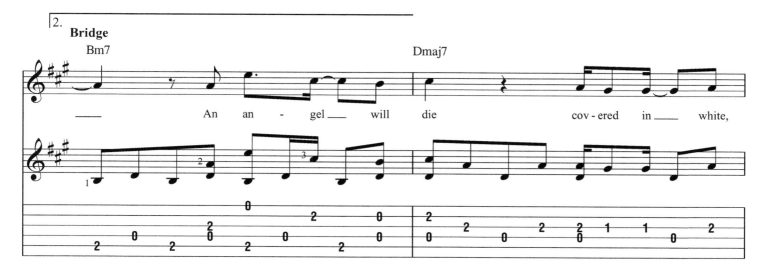

An an - gel ___ will die cov - ered in ___ white,

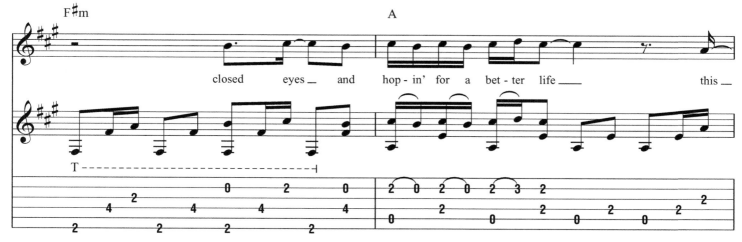

closed eyes ___ and hop - in' for a bet - ter life ___ this ___

D.S. al Coda
(take 1st ending)

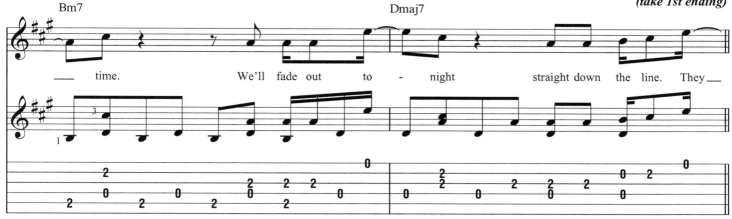

___ time. We'll fade out to - night straight down the line. They ___

Coda

An - gels ___ to die. ___

Creep

Words and Music by Albert Hammond, Mike Hazlewood, Thomas Yorke, Jonathan Greenwood, Colin Greenwood, Edward O'Brien and Philip Selway

Chorus

I'm a _____ wierd - o. _____

What the hell ___ am I do-ing here? ___   I don't be - long ___

|1.   *To Coda* ⊕ |2.

___ here.   2. I don't care if it hurts. ___ ___ here.   Oh, ___

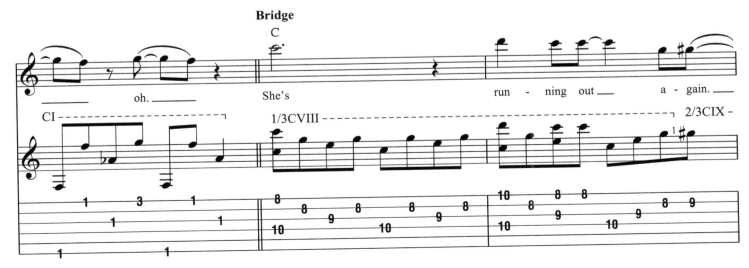

Bridge

oh. ___   She's   run - ning out ___ a - gain. ___

12

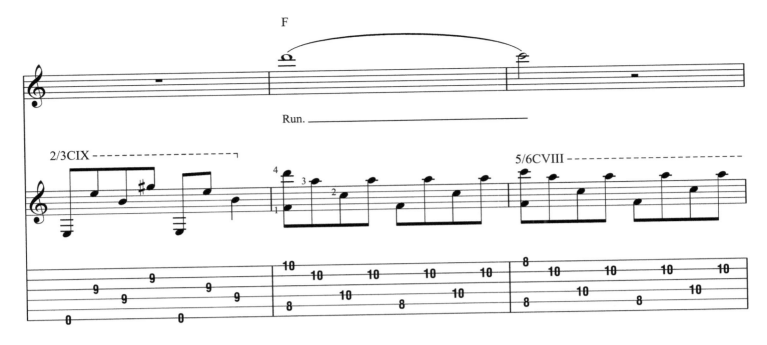

F

Run.

2/3CIX

5/6CVIII

D.S. al Coda
(take 1st ending)

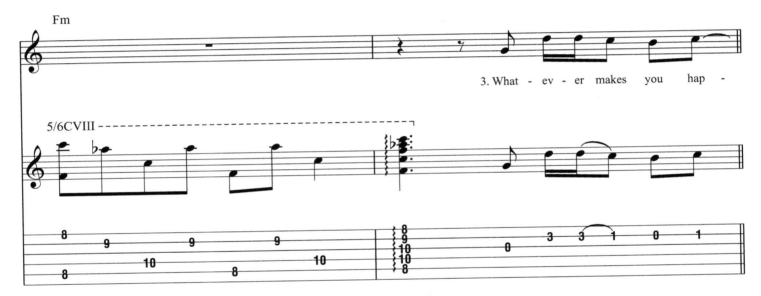

Fm

3. What - ev - er makes you hap -

5/6CVIII

⊕ **Coda**

C

rit.

I don't be - long _____ here.

CI

rit.

Daughters

Words and Music by John Mayer

Verse

Slow

1. I _____ know a girl; _____ she puts the col-

-or in-side of my world. _____ But she's just like a

maze _____ where all of the walls _____ all con-tin-u'l-ly change. _____ And

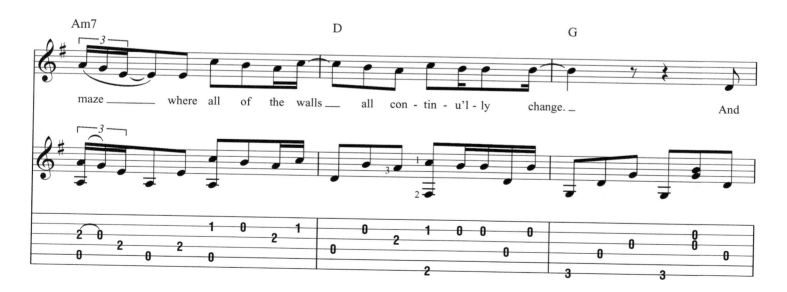

Girls be - come _ lov - ers who turn in - to moth - ers. So, moth - ers, be good _ to your

Verse

daugh - ters, _ too. 2. Oh, ___ you see that skin? _____ It's the same _

_ she's been stand - ing in _____ since _ the day she saw him

17

walk - ing a - way. Now she's left   clean-ing up the mess he made.   So,

⊕ Coda 1

Bridge

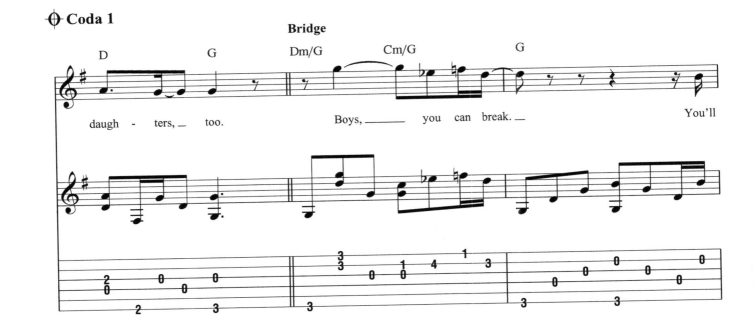

daugh - ters, ___ too.   Boys, _____ you can break. ___   You'll

find out how much ___ they can take. ___   Boys will be   strong, ___   and boys sol - dier on. ___

18

But boys would be gone — with - out warmth from a wom - an's

Interlude

good, good heart.

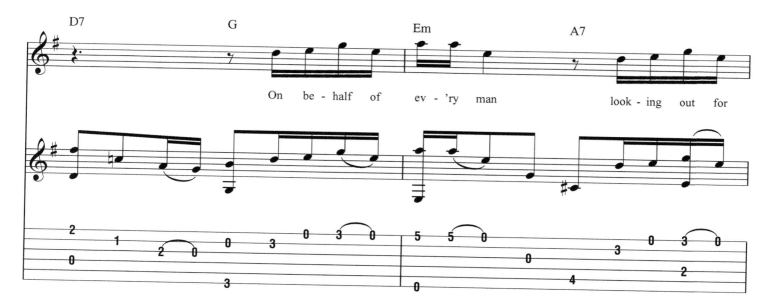

On be - half of ev - 'ry man look - ing out for

19

ev - 'ry girl, you are the god and the weight __ of her world. __ So,

⊕ Coda 2

daugh - ters, __ too. So, moth - ers, be good __ to your daugh - ters, __ too. So,

moth - ers, be good ___ to your ___ daugh - ters, too.

20

Elderly Woman Behind the Counter in a Small Town

Words by Eddie Vedder
Music by Eddie Vedder, Jeff Ament, Stone Gossard, Mike McCready and Dave Abbruzzese

Drop D tuning:
(low to high) D-A-D-G-B-E

Verse
Moderately

1. I seem to rec-og-nize your face. ____

Haunt - ing, fa - mil - iar, yet I can't seem to ____ place it. ____

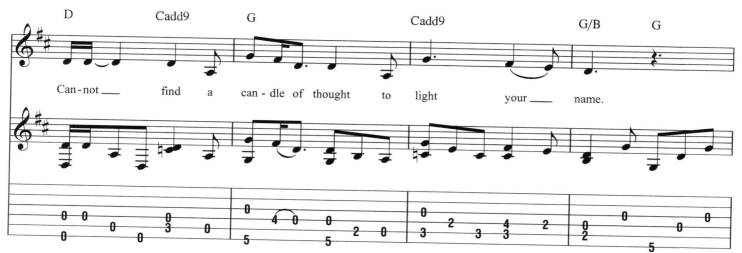

Can-not ____ find a can-dle of thought to light your ____ name.

24

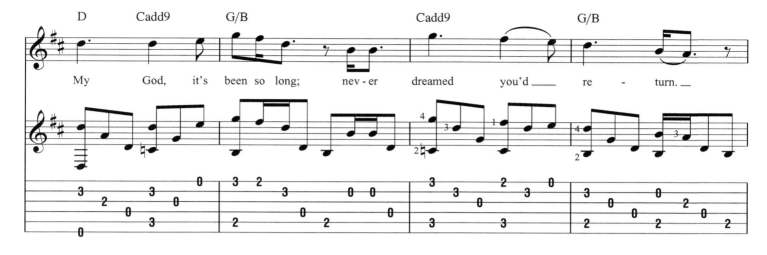

My God, it's been so long; nev-er dreamed you'd __ re - turn. __

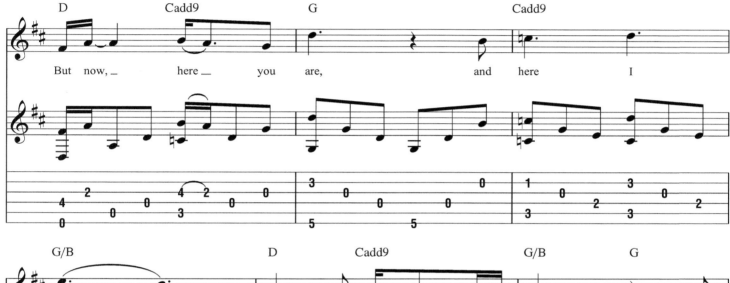

But now, __ here __ you are, and here I

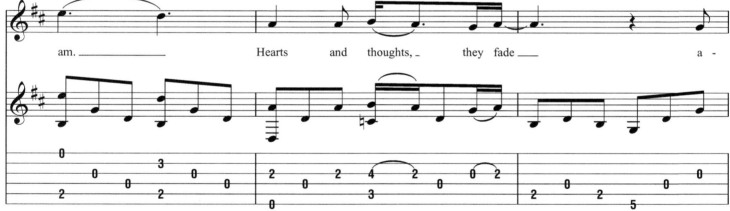

am. _____ Hearts and thoughts, _ they fade __ a -

D.S. al Coda   **⊕ Coda**

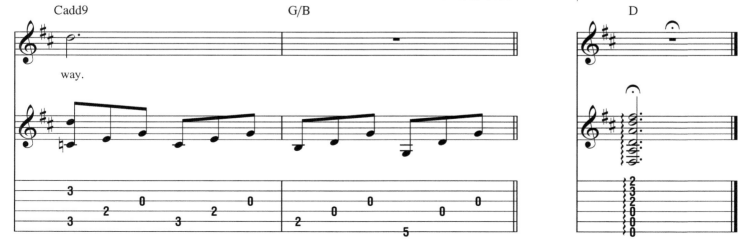

way.

Everybody Hurts

Words and Music by William Berry, Peter Buck, Michael Mills and Michael Stipe

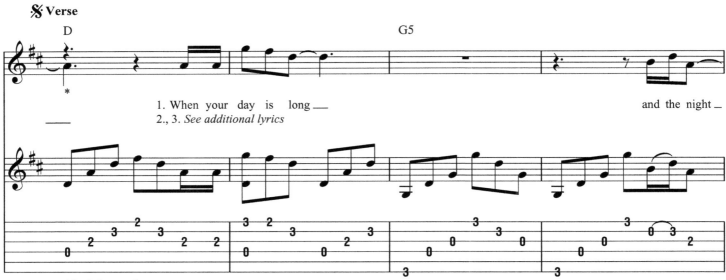

1. When your day is long ___ and the night ___

2., 3. *See additional lyrics*

*2nd time only.

the night is yours ___ a-lone. ___

When you're sure you've had e - nough of this life, __

__ well, hang on. ____

Chorus

Don't let your - self go, ____

'cause ev - 'ry - bod-y cries. ____

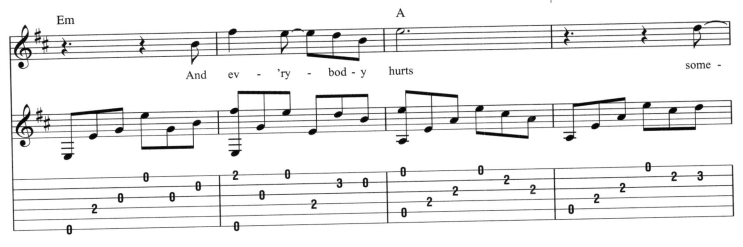

When you feel like _____ you're a - lone, _____

D.S. al Coda 2

no,   no,   no,   you are not a - lone. _____

⊕ Coda 2

- times. _____

So hold _____ on. _____

rit.

rit.

Additional Lyrics

2. When your day is night alone.
   If you feel like letting go.
   If you think you've had too much of this life,
   Well, hang on.

Chorus: 'Cause ev'rybody hurts.
   Take comfort in your friends.
   Ev'rybody hurts.

3. If you're on your own in this life,
   The days and nights are long.
   When you think you've had too much of this life,
   To hang on.

Chorus: Well, ev'rybody hurts.
   Sometimes ev'rybody cries.
   Ev'rybody hurts sometimes.

Fast Car

Words and Music by Tracy Chapman

Intro
Moderately

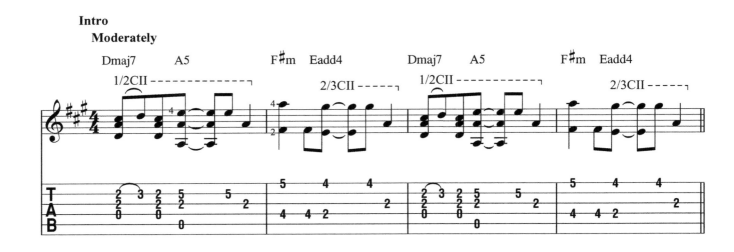

Verse

1. You got a fast ____ car. I want a tick-et to an-y-where.
2.–7. *See additional lyrics*

4th time, skip to Interlude

7th time, To Coda ⊕

May-be we make a deal; ___ may-be to-geth-er we can get some-where. ___

An - y place is bet - ter. ___ Start - ing from ze - ro, got noth - ing to lose.

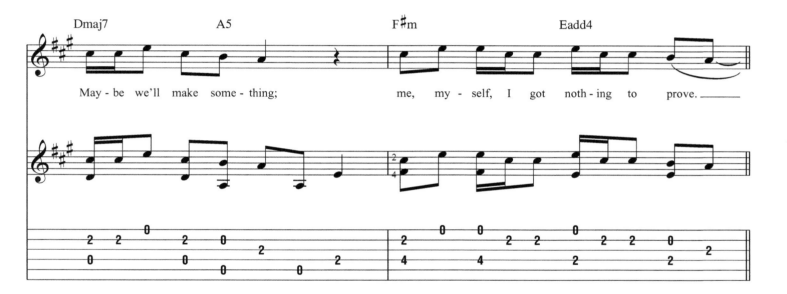

May - be we'll make some - thing; me, my - self, I got noth - ing to prove. _____

Interlude

[1., 2., 3.]

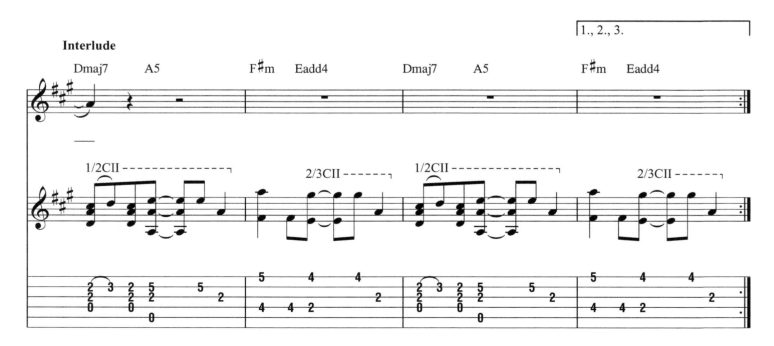

Chorus

I re - mem - ber when we were driv - ing, driv - ing in your car, __ the

speed so fast __ I felt like __ I was drunk. Cit - y lights lay out be - fore __ us; your

arm felt nice wrapped 'round my shoul - der and I _____ had a

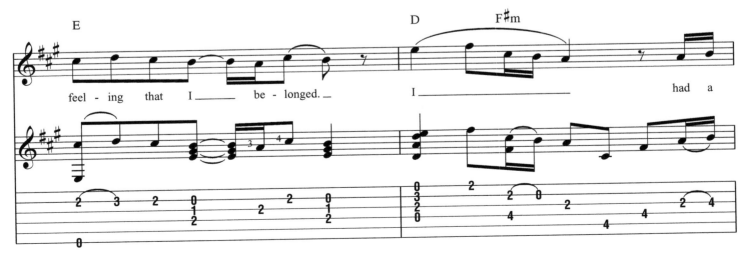

feel - ing that I ____ be - longed. __ I _____ had a

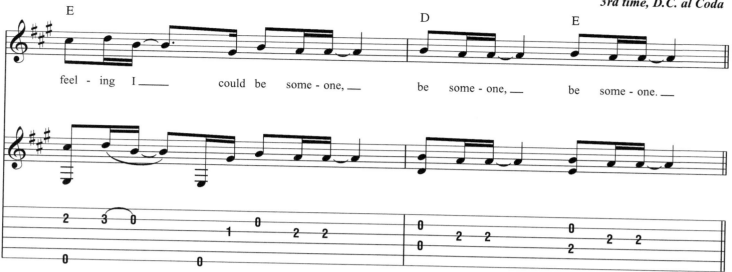

feel - ing I ____ could be some - one, ____ be some - one, ____ be some - one. ____

Coda

Outro

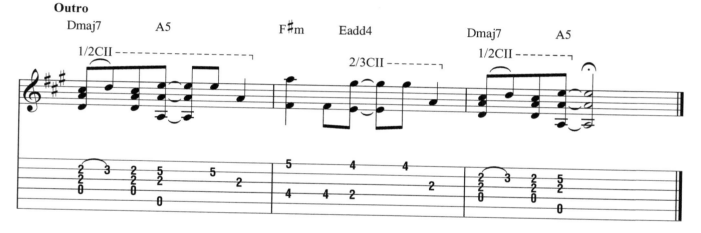

Additional Lyrics

2. You got a fast car.
   I got a plan to get us out of here.
   Been working at the convenience store,
   Managed to save just a little bit of money.
   Won't have to drive too far,
   Just cross the border and into the city.
   You and I can both get jobs,
   Finally see what it means to be living.

3. You see, my old man's got a problem.
   He live with the bottle, that's the way it is.
   He says his body's too old for working;
   His body's too young to look like his.
   My mama went off and left him;
   She wanted more from life than he could give.
   I said somebody's got to take care of him.
   So I quit school and that's what I did.

4. You got a fast car,
   But is it fast enough so we can fly away?
   We gotta make a decision:
   Leave tonight or live and die this way.
   (To Interlude)

5. You got a fast car.
   We go cruising to entertain ourselves.
   You still ain't got a job
   And I work in the market as a checkout girl.
   I know things will get better;
   You'll find work and I'll get promoted.
   We'll move out of the shelter,
   Buy a big house and live in the suburbs.

6. You got a fast car.
   I got a job that pays all our bills.
   You stay out drinking late at the bar,
   See more of your friends than you do of your kids.
   I'd always hoped for better,
   Thought maybe together you and me'd find it.
   I got no plans, I ain't going nowhere,
   So take your fast car and keep on driving.

7. You got a fast car.
   Is it fast enough so you can fly away?
   You gotta make a decision:
   Leave tonight or live and die this way.

Hey There Delilah

Words and Music by Tom Higgenson

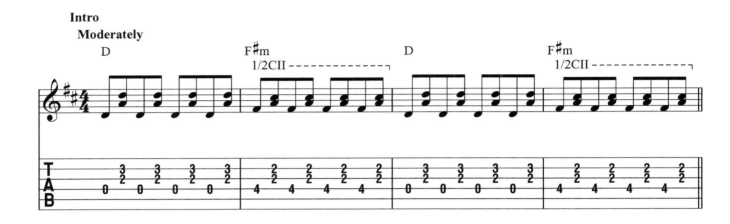

1. Hey there, De - li - lah, what's it like in New York Cit - y? I'm a
2. *See additional lyrics*

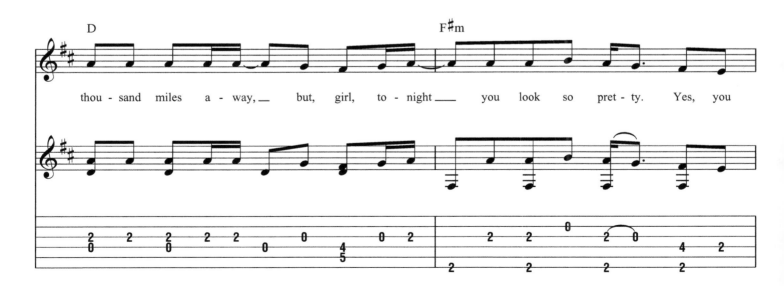

thou - sand miles a - way, __ but, girl, to - night __ you look so pret - ty. Yes, you

Our friends would all ___ make fun of us, ___ and

we'll just laugh a - long ___ be - cause ___ we know that none of them ___ have felt ___ this

way. De - li - lah, I ___ can prom - ise you ___ that

by the time __ that we get through __ the world __ will nev-er ev-er be the same, __

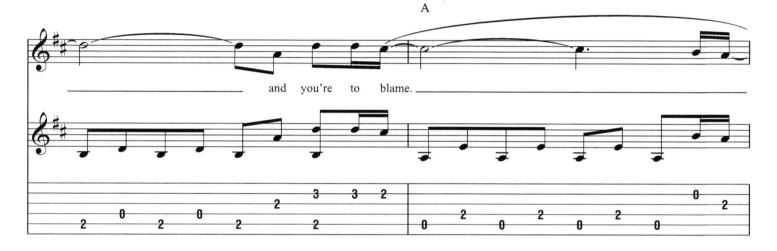

____ and you're to blame. _____

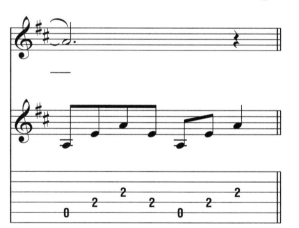

D.S. al Coda
(take 1st ending)

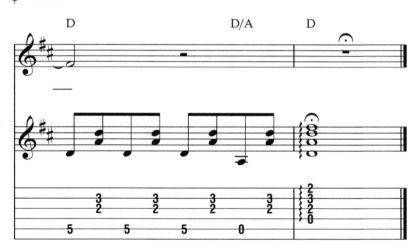

⊕ **Coda**

Additional Lyrics

2. Hey there, Delilah, I know times are gettin' hard.
   But just believe me, girl, someday I'll pay the bills with this guitar.
   We'll have it good.
   We'll have the life we knew we would; my word is good.
   Hey there, Delilah, I've got so much left to say.
   If every simple song I wrote to you would take your breath away,
   I'd write it all.
   Even more in love with me you'd fall; we'd have it all.

3. Hey there, Delilah, you be good and don't you miss me.
   Two more years and you'll be done with school, and I'll me making history like I do.
   You know it's all because of you.

I Will Follow You Into the Dark

Words and Music by Benjamin Gibbard

Intro
Moderately

Verse

1. Love of ___ mine, some day you will ___ die, but I'll be
2., 3. *See additional lyrics*

close be - hind. I'll fol - low you ___ in - to the dark. ___ No

*T=Thumb on 6th string

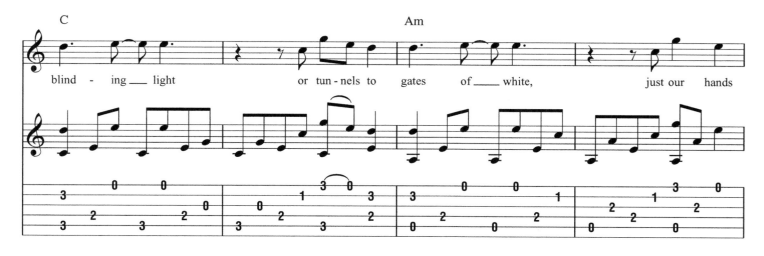

blind - ing ___ light   or tun - nels to gates of ___ white,   just our hands

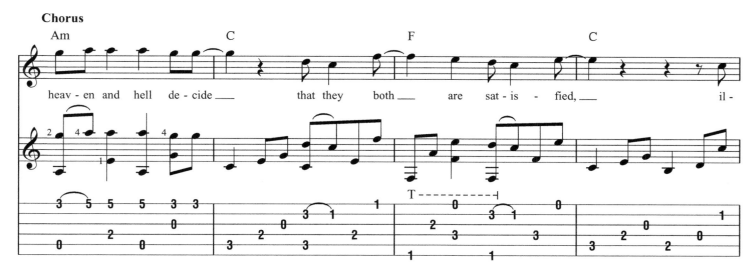

clasped so ___ tight   wait - ing for ___ the hint of a spark. ___   If

Chorus

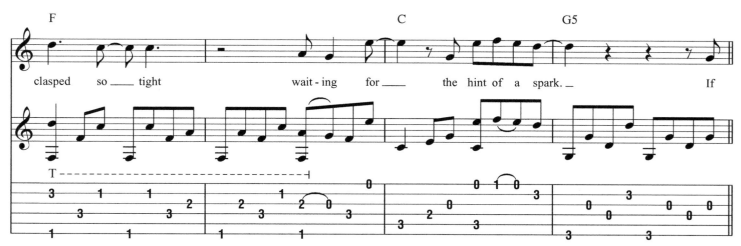

heav - en and hell de - cide ___   that they both ___ are sat - is - fied, ___   il -

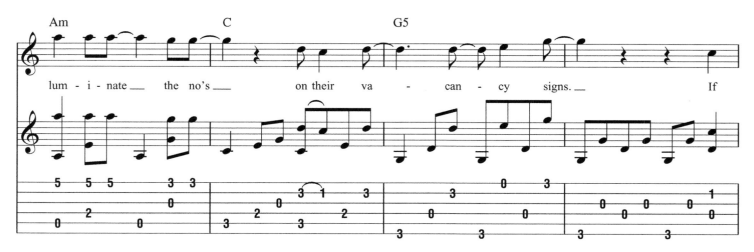

lum - i - nate ___ the no's ___   on their va - can - cy signs. ___   If

there's no one be-side___ you   when your___ soul em - barks,___   then

I'll fol - low you___ in - to the dark.   2. In

And I'll fol - low you___ in - to the dark.

Additional Lyrics

2. In Catholic school, as vicious as Roman rule,
   I got my knuckles bruised by a lady in black.
   And I held my tongue as she told me, "Son,
   Fear is the heart of love." So I never went back.

3. You and me have seen everything to see
   From Bangkok to Calgary, and the soles of your shoes
   Are all worn down; the time for sleep is now.
   But it's nothing to cry about,
   'Cause we'll hold each other soon.

I Won't Give Up

Words and Music by Jason Mraz and Michael Natter

Drop D tuning:
(low to high) D-A-D-G-B-E

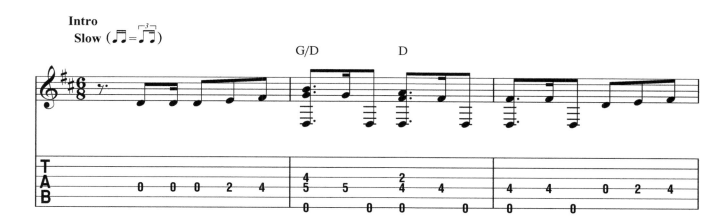

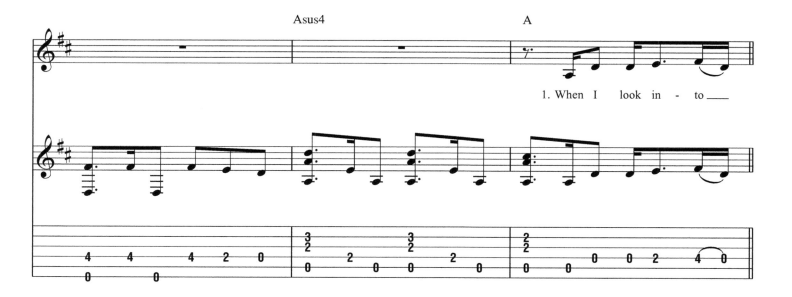

Chorus

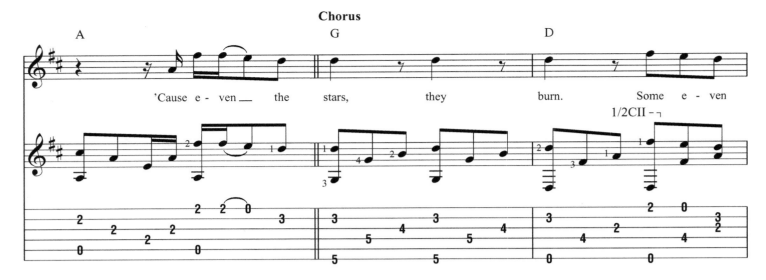

'Cause e - ven the stars, they burn. Some e - ven

fall to the earth. We got a lot to

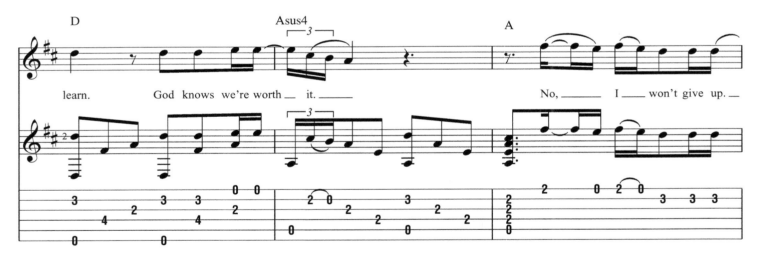

learn. God knows we're worth it. No, I won't give up.

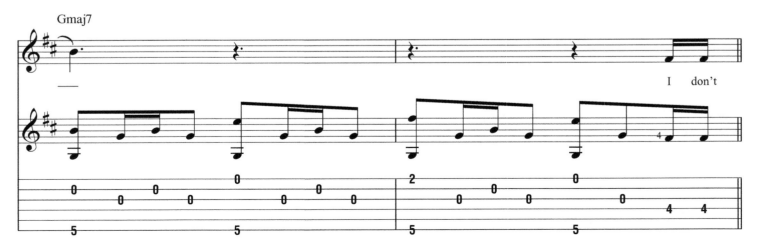

I don't

Bridge

wan - na be some-one who walks a - way so eas - i - ly. I'm here to stay and make the dif - fer - ence that

I can make. _____ Our

dif - f'renc - es, they do a lot to teach us how to use the tools and gifts we got. Yeah, we got a lot _

_____ at stake. _____ And in the

end, you're still my friend; at least we did in-tend for us to work. We did-n't break; we did-n't burn.

We had to learn how to bend with-out the world cav-ing in.

I had to learn what I got ___ and what I'm not and who I

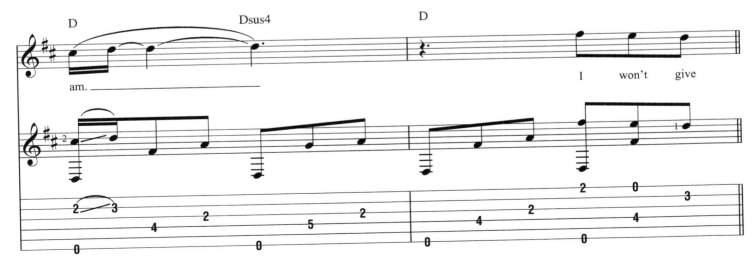

am. ___

I won't give

Chorus

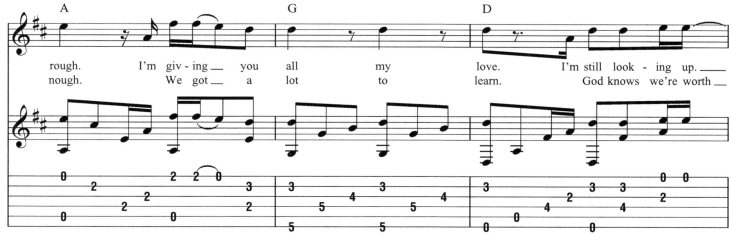

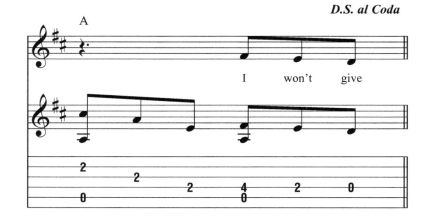

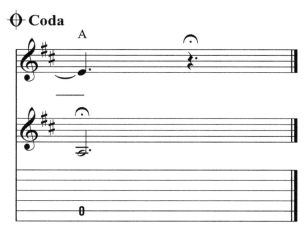

Iris

from the Motion Picture CITY OF ANGELS
Words and Music by John Rzeznik

― ev - er be, and I don't wan - na go ― home right now. 2. And all ―

Verse

― I can taste ― is this mo - ment,
― fight the tears ― that ain't com - ing,
and all ― I can breathe ― is your life. ―
or the mo - ment of truth ― in your lies. ―

― Well, soon - er or lat - er, it's o - ver. I just
― When ev - 'ry - thing feels ― like the mov - ies, yeah, you

don't wan - na miss ― you to - night. ―
bleed just to know ― you're a - live. ―
And I

Chorus

don't want the world _____ to see _____ me _____ 'cause I don't think that they'd ___ un - der -

stand. When ev - 'ry - thing's made to be bro - ken, I just

To Coda ⊕

Interlude

want you to know ___ who I am.

52

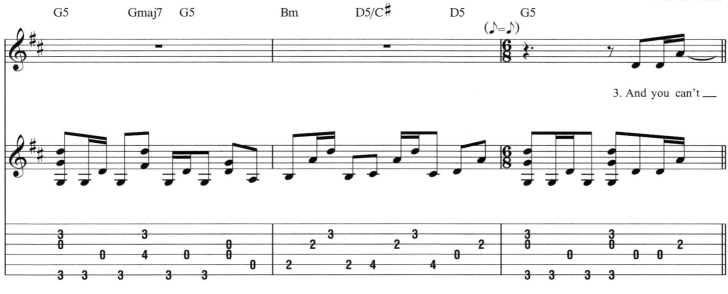

Coda

Outro

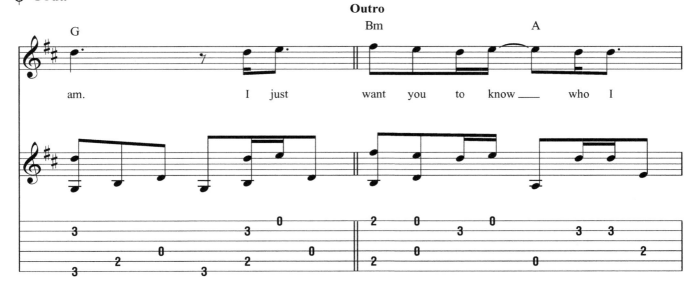

My Friends

Words and Music by Anthony Kiedis, Flea, Chad Smith and David Navarro

You know I will. ____

I love

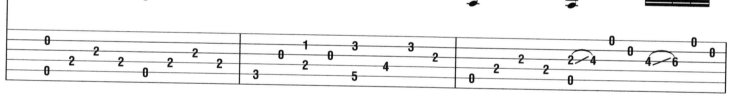

all of you ____ hurt by the cold. ____

To Coda 1 ⊕
To Coda 2 ⊕

So hard and lone - ly, too, ____ when you don't know ____

D.S. al Coda 1
(take 3rd ending)

Coda 1

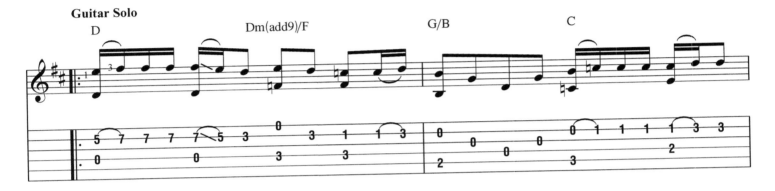

Guitar Solo

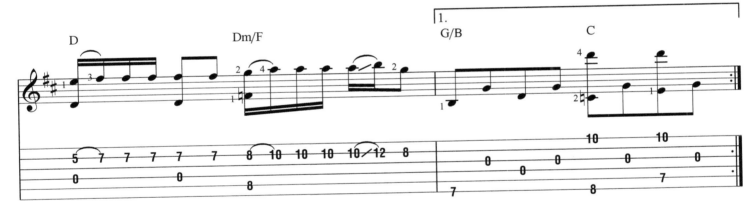

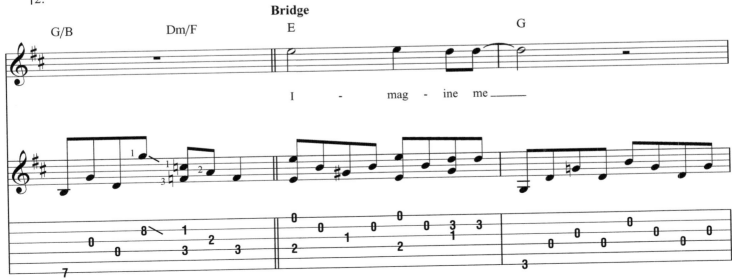

D.S. al Coda 2
(take 4th ending)

Coda 2

Outro

Additional Lyrics

2. Ex-girlfriend called me up
Alone and desperate on a prison phone.
They want to give her seven years
For being sad.

3. My friends are so distressed.
They're standing on the brink of emptiness.
No words I know of to express
This emptiness.

4. I heard a little girl
And what she said was something beautiful.
To give your love no matter what
Is what she said.

To Be with You

Words and Music by Eric Martin and David Grahame

Verse
Moderately slow

1. Hold on, ___ lit - tle girl. ___ Show me what ___ he's done to you. ___
2. *See additional lyrics*

Stand up, ___ lit - tle girl. ___ A bro - ken heart ___ can't be that bad. ___ When

it's through, ___ it's through. ___ Fate will twist ___ the both ___ of you. ___ So,

come on, ba - by, come on o - ver. Let me be ___ the one ___ to show you.

Chorus

I'm the one who wants to be with you. ___ Deep in - side I hope you

feel ___ it, too. ___ Wait - ed on a line of greens and blues. ___

Just to be the next to be _____ with you. _____

Bridge

Why be a - lone when we can be to - geth - er, ba - by?

You can make _ my life _ worth - while. _   I can make _ you start _ to

60

Guitar Solo

smile.

D.S. al Coda
(take 1st lyrics)

When

✪ **Coda**

Just to be the next to _____ be with you. _____

Additional Lyrics

2. Build up your confidence
So you can be on top for once.
Wake up; who cares about
Little boys that talk too much?
I've seen it all go down.
Your game of love was all rained out.
So, come on, baby, come on over.
Let me be the one to hold you.

Sunny Came Home

Words and Music by Shawn Colvin and John Leventhal

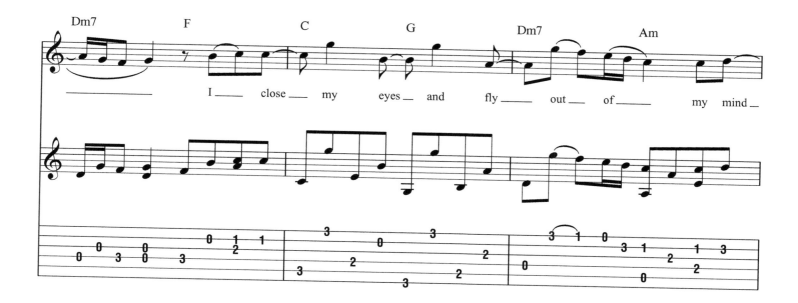

list of names. ____ She did-n't be-lieve ____ in tran - scen - dence.

"And it's time for a few small re - pairs," she ____ said. ____ Sun - ny came home with a

D.S. al Coda   **⊕ Coda**

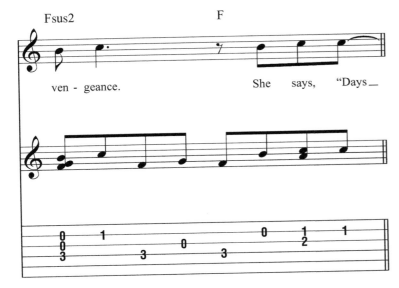

ven - geance.   She says, "Days ____

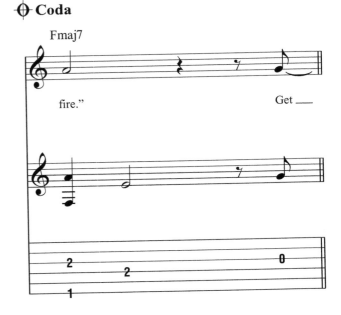

fire."   Get ____

Bridge

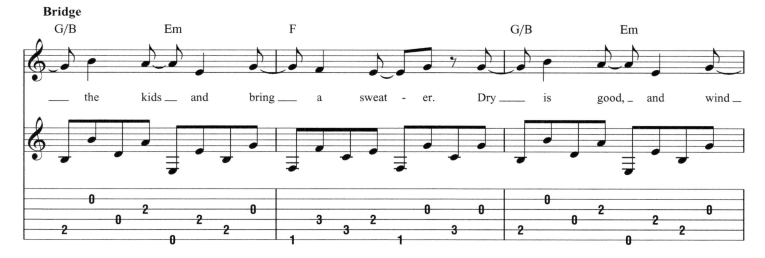

the kids — and bring — a sweat - er. Dry — is good, — and wind —

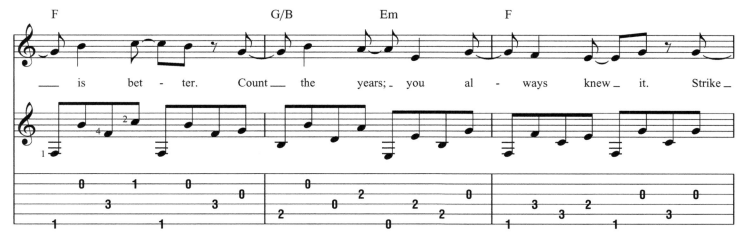

— is bet - ter. Count — the years; — you al - ways knew — it. Strike —

Chorus

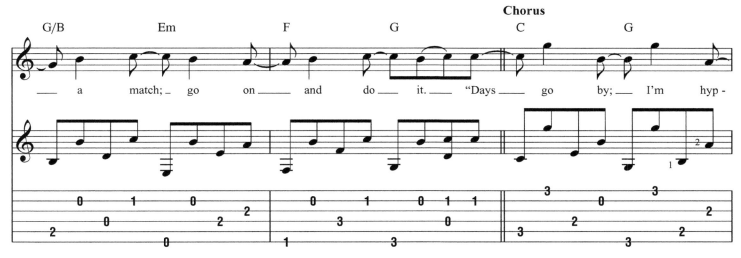

— a match; — go on — and do — it. — "Days — go by; — I'm hyp -

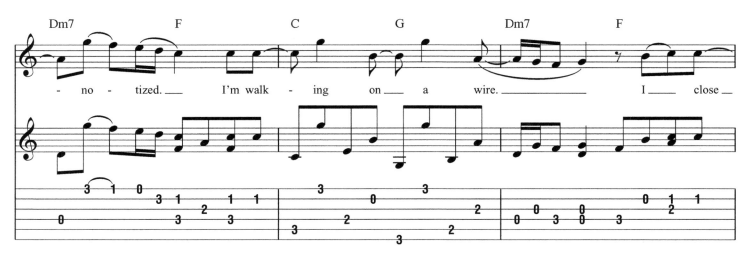

- no - tized. — I'm walk - ing on a wire. — I close —

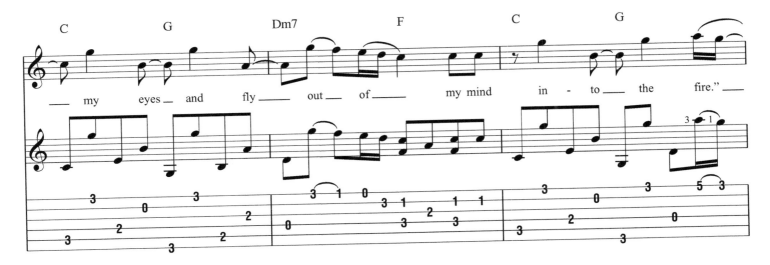

Outro-Chorus

Wake Me Up When September Ends

Words by Billie Joe
Music by Green Day

Intro
Moderately

1. Sum - mer __ has   come and passed; __   the in - no - cent __ can nev -
3., 5. *See additional lyrics*

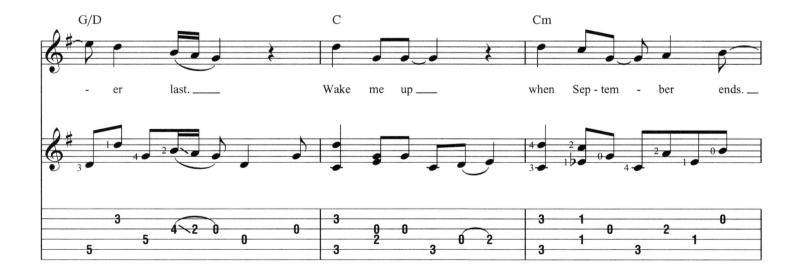

- er last. __   Wake me up __   when Sep - tem - ber ends. __

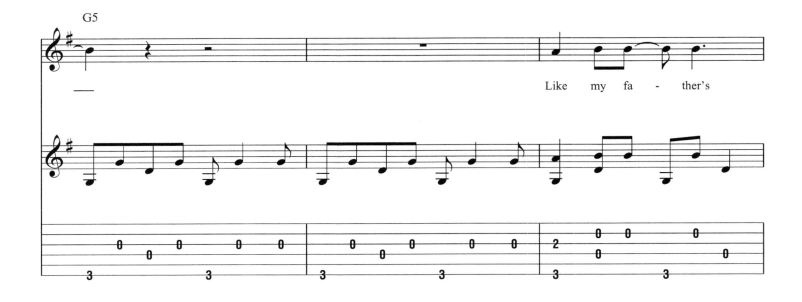

Like my fa - ther's

come to pass, ____ sev - en years ____ has gone ____ so fast. ____

To Coda ⊕

Wake me up ____ when Sep - tem - ber ends. ____

Chorus

Verse

2. As my mem - o - ry rests, but nev - er for - gets what
4. *See additional lyrics*

I lost. Wake me up when Sep - tem - ber ends.

D.S. al Coda

⊕ Coda

Outro

Wake me up ___ when Sep - tem - ber ends. ___

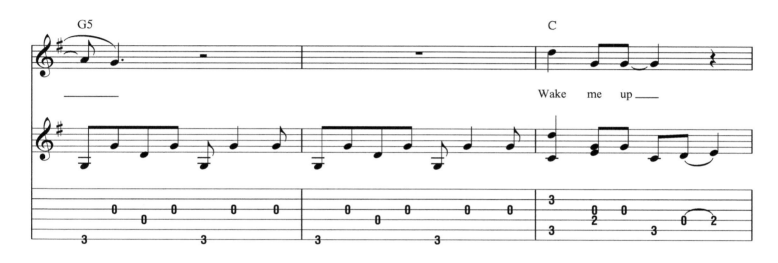

___ Wake me up ___

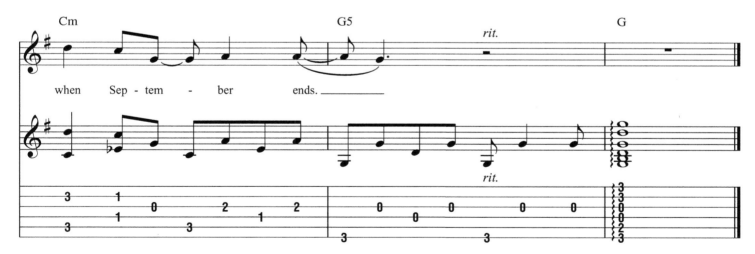

when Sep - tem - ber ends. ___

Additional Lyrics

3. Summer has come and passed; the innocent can never last.
   Wake me up when September ends.
   Ring out the bells again, like we did when Spring began.
   Wake me up when September ends.

4. As my memory rests, but never forgets what I lost.
   Wake me up when September ends.

5. Summer has come and passed; the innocent can never last.
   Wake me up when September ends.
   Like my father's come to pass, twenty years has gone so fast.
   Wake me up when September ends.

Wonderwall

Words and Music by Noel Gallagher

I don't be - lieve _ that an - y - bod - y feels the way I do _ a - bout you now. _

Verse

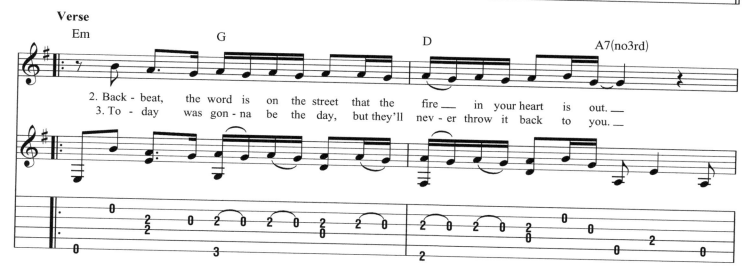

2. Back - beat, the word is on the street that the fire _ in your heart is out. _
3. To - day was gon - na be the day, but they'll nev - er throw it back to you. _

I'm sure you've heard it all be - fore, but you nev - er real - ly had a doubt. _
By now, you should have some - how re - al - ized what you're not to do. _

I don't be - lieve __ that an - y - bod - y feels the way I do __ a - bout you now. __

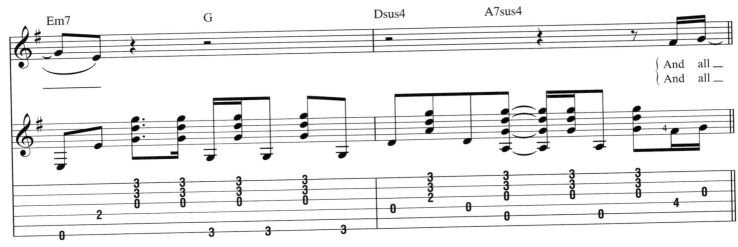

{ And all __
{ And all __

Pre-Chorus

__ the roads __ we have __ to walk __ are wind - ing,
__ the roads __ that lead __ you there __ were wind - ing,

and all __
and all __

__ the lights __ that lead __ us there __ are blind - ing. }
__ the lights __ that light __ the way __ are blind - ing. }

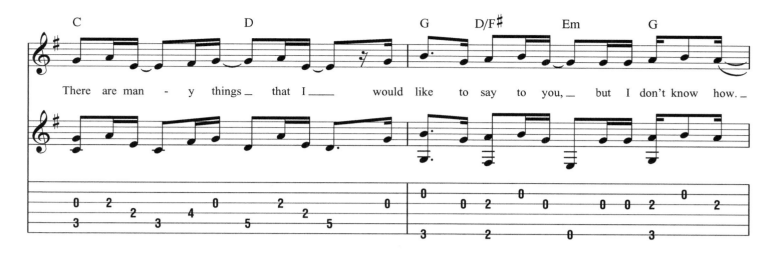

There are man - y things _ that I _ would like to say to you, _ but I don't know how. _

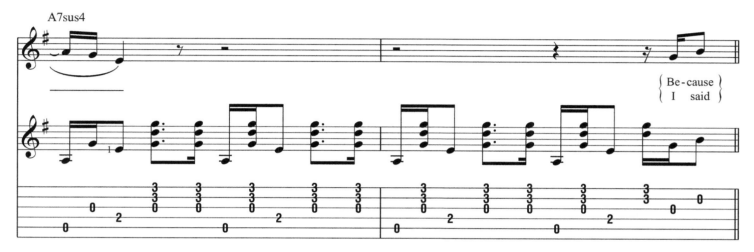

{ Be - cause }
{ I said }

𝄋 Chorus

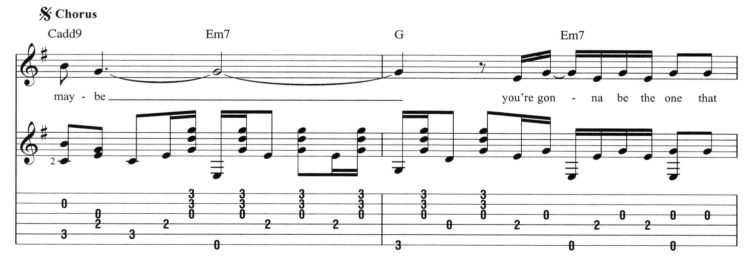

may - be _ you're gon - na be the one that

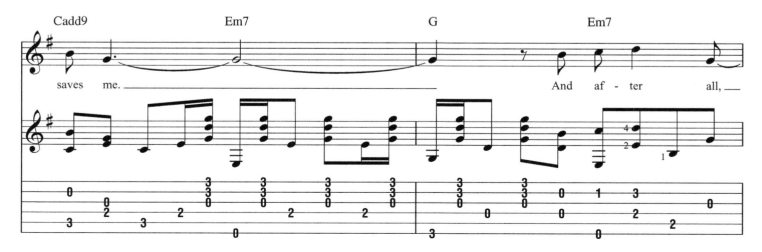

saves me. _ And af - ter all, _

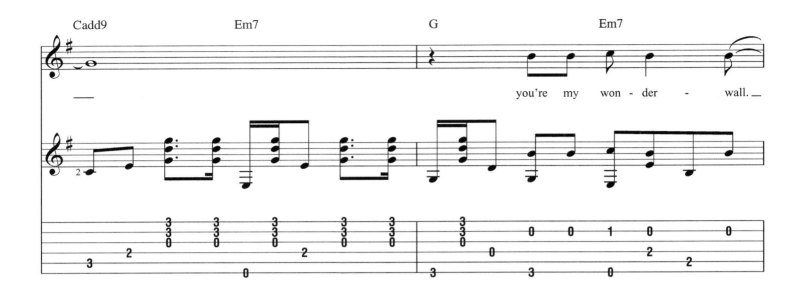

you're my won - der - wall. __

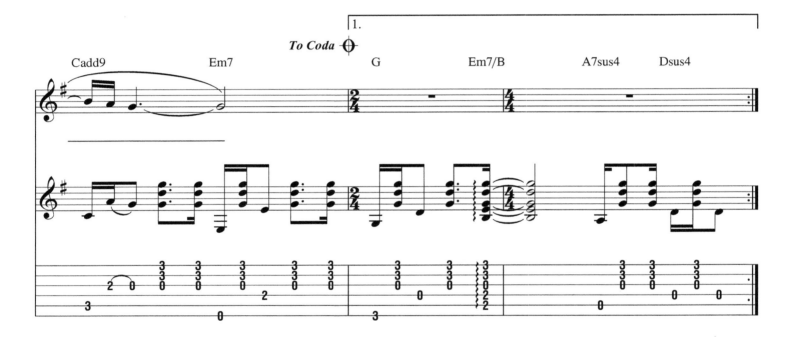

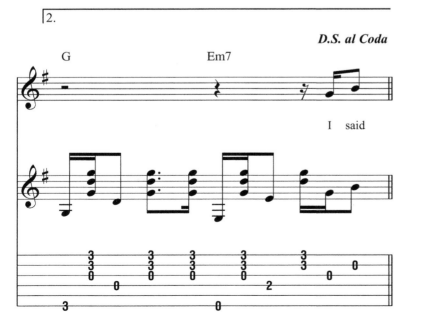

I said

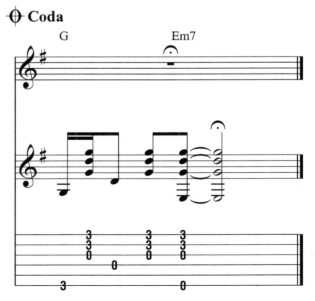

   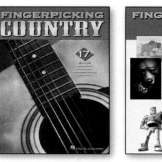

AUTHENTIC CHORDS • ORIGINAL KEYS • COMPLETE SONGS

The *Strum It* series lets players strum the chords and sing along with their favorite hits. Each song has been selected because it can be played with regular open chords, barre chords, or other moveable chord types. Guitarists can simply play the rhythm, or play and sing along through the entire song. All songs are shown in their original keys complete with chords, strum patterns, melody and lyrics. Wherever possible, the chord voicings from the recorded versions are notated.

THE BEACH BOYS' GREATEST HITS
00699357.............................$12.95

THE BEATLES FAVORITES
00699249.............................$15.99

VERY BEST OF JOHNNY CASH
00699514.............................$14.99

CELTIC GUITAR SONGBOOK
00699265.............................$12.99

CHRISTMAS SONGS FOR GUITAR
00699247.............................$10.95

CHRISTMAS SONGS WITH 3 CHORDS
00699487.............................$9.99

VERY BEST OF ERIC CLAPTON
00699560.............................$12.95

JIM CROCE – CLASSIC HITS
00699269.............................$10.95

DISNEY FAVORITES
00699171.............................$14.99

MELISSA ETHERIDGE GREATEST HITS
00699518.............................$12.99

FAVORITE SONGS WITH 3 CHORDS
00699112.............................$10.99

FAVORITE SONGS WITH 4 CHORDS
00699270.............................$8.95

FIRESIDE SING-ALONG
00699273.............................$12.99

FOLK FAVORITES
00699517.............................$8.95

THE GUITAR STRUMMERS' ROCK SONGBOOK
00701678.............................$14.99

BEST OF WOODY GUTHRIE
00699496.............................$12.95

JOHN HIATT COLLECTION
00699398.............................$17.99

THE VERY BEST OF BOB MARLEY
00699524.............................$14.99

A MERRY CHRISTMAS SONGBOOK
00699211.............................$10.99

MORE FAVORITE SONGS WITH 3 CHORDS
00699532.............................$9.99

THE VERY BEST OF TOM PETTY
00699336.............................$15.99

BEST OF GEORGE STRAIT
00699235.............................$16.99

TAYLOR SWIFT FOR ACOUSTIC GUITAR
00109717.............................$16.99

BEST OF HANK WILLIAMS JR.
00699224.............................$16.99

HAL•LEONARD®

Visit Hal Leonard online at
www.halleonard.com

Prices, contents & availability subject to change without notice.

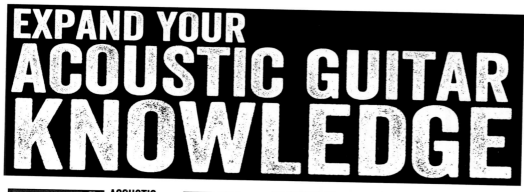

EXPAND YOUR ACOUSTIC GUITAR KNOWLEDGE

ACOUSTIC GUITAR CHORDS
INCLUDES TAB · DVD

by Chad Johnson

In any music style, there are essentials – scales, licks, chords, etc. This book teaches you the must-know chords that will get you strumming quickly. Rather, you'll be armed with many chord shapes that have been used throughout the acoustic guitar's history in countless hits. The included DVD demonstrates each chord and all the examples are accompanied by a full band.

00696484 Book/DVD Pack............................$9.99

ACOUSTIC GUITAR LESSON PACK
INCLUDES TAB · DVD

This boxed set includes four books (*Acoustic Guitar Method, Guitar Chord Chart, Guitar Scale Chart,* and *Guitar Theory*) and the *200 Acoustic Licks* DVD that includes tasty lead lines and fingerstyle phrases, creative riffs, walk-through explanations by pro guitarists, note-for-note on-screen tablature; normal- and slow-speed performance demos.

00131554 4 Books & 1 DVD........................$29.99

FIRST 15 LESSONS – ACOUSTIC GUITAR
INCLUDES TAB

by Troy Nelson

The First 15 Lessons series provides a step-by-step lesson plan for the absolute beginner, complete with audio tracks, video lessons, and real songs! The acoustic guitar book, features lessons on: guitar fundamentals, chords, strumming, arpeggios, time signatures, syncopation, hammer-ons & pull-offs, double stops, harmonics, fingerpicking, alternate picking, and scales & basic theory.

00696484 Book/Online Media........................$9.99

THE HAL LEONARD ACOUSTIC GUITAR METHOD
INCLUDES TAB

by Chad Johnson

This method uses real songs to teach you all the basics of acoustic guitar in the style of the Beatles, Eric Clapton, John Mellencamp, James Taylor and many others. Lessons include: strumming; fingerpicking; using a capo; open tunings; folk, country & bluegrass styles; acoustic blues; acoustic rock; and more.

00697347 Book/Online Audio........................$17.99

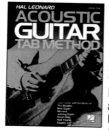

THE HAL LEONARD ACOUSTIC GUITAR TAB METHOD
INCLUDES TAB

Learn chords with songs like "Eleanor Rigby" and "Knockin' on Heaven's Door," single notes with riffs and solos by Nirvana and Pink Floyd, arpeggios with classics by Eric Clapton and Boston, and more. This method's well-paced, logical teaching sequence will get students playing more easily than ever before, and music from popular artists like the Eagles, Johnny Cash & Green Day keeps them playing and having fun.

00124197 Book/Online Audio........................$12.99
00146365 Book Only................................$6.99

HAL LEONARD FINGERSTYLE GUITAR METHOD
INCLUDES TAB

by Chad Johnson

The *Hal Leonard Fingerstyle Guitar Method* is your complete guide to learning fingerstyle guitar. Songs covered include: Annie's Song • Blowin' in the Wind • Dust in the Wind • Fire and Rain • Georgia on My Mind • Imagine • Landslide • Tears in Heaven • What a Wonderful World • Yesterday • You've Got a Friend • and more.

00697378 Book/Online Audio........................$21.99

HOW TO FINGERPICK SONGS ON GUITAR
INCLUDES TAB

by Chad Johnson

Learn fingerstyle techniques from the ground up with exercises, songs, and videos designed to lead you into a whole new world of guitar enjoyment. Along the way, you will also explore how to create solo-guitar arrangements of your favorite songs using a variety of methods. Plus every technique, topic, playing example, and song in the book is demonstrated for you on video!

00155364 Book/Online Video........................$14.99

HAL•LEONARD®

www.halleonard.com

Prices, contents, and availability subject to change without notice.

100 ACOUSTIC LESSONS
INCLUDES TAB

by Chad Johnson and Michael Mueller

Featuring 100 individual modules covering a giant array of topics, each lesson in this Acoustic volume includes detailed instruction with playing examples presented in standard notation and tablature. You'll also get extremely useful tips, scale diagrams, chord grids, photos, and more to reinforce your learning experience, plus online audio with performance demos of examples in the book!

00696456 Book/Online Audio........................$24.99

PERCUSSIVE ACOUSTIC GUITAR METHOD
INCLUDES TAB

by Chris Woods

Providing detailed, step-by-step instruction on a variety of percussive guitar techniques, this book includes warm-ups, exercises, full peices, and pracitcal "how-to" training that will get you slapping and tapping. Covers: string slapping, body percussion, tapping, harmonics, alternate tunings, standard notation & tab, and more!

00696643 Book/Online Video........................$19.99

PLAY ACOUSTIC GUITAR IN MINUTES

by Andrew DuBrock

This fantastic beginner's guide will get your fingers on the fretboard in no time! You'll quickly learn easy chords, basic fingerpicking, strumming patterns, chord progressions, and much more. The online video features over 2 hours of instruction with Andrew DuBrock himself as your personal teacher, reinforcing all the lessons in the book.

00696621 Book/Online Video........................$21.99

TOTAL ACOUSTIC GUITAR
INCLUDES TAB

by Andrew DuBrock

Packed with tons of examples and audio demonstrations, this book/online audio package breaks down the most common, essential acoustic techniques with clear, concise instruction and then applies them to real-world musical riffs, licks, and songs. You'll learn syncopation, power chords, arpeggios, rhythm fills, and much more.

00696072 Book/Online Audio........................$19.99

TRAVIS PICKING
INCLUDES TAB

by Andrew DuBrock

From the backwoods of Kentucky to modern-day concert arenas, the Travis picking technique has been a guitar staple for generations. In this guide, you'll go step-by-step from basic accompaniment patterns to advanced fingerpicking methods in the style of Merle, Chet and others.

00696425 Book/Online Audio........................$16.99

FINGERPICKING GUITAR BOOKS

Hone your fingerpicking skills with these great songbooks featuring solo guitar arrangements in standard notation and tablature. The arrangements in these books are carefully written for intermediate-level guitarists. Each song combines melody and harmony in one superb guitar fingerpicking arrangement. Each book also includes an introduction to basic fingerstyle guitar.

FINGERPICKING ACOUSTIC
00699614...$12.99

FINGERPICKING ACOUSTIC CLASSICS
00160211...$12.99

FINGERPICKING ACOUSTIC HITS
00160202...$12.99

FINGERPICKING ACOUSTIC ROCK
00699764...$12.99

FINGERPICKING BALLADS
00699717...$12.99

FINGERPICKING BEATLES
00699049...$19.99

FINGERPICKING BEETHOVEN
00702390...$7.99

FINGERPICKING BLUES
00701277...$9.99

FINGERPICKING BROADWAY FAVORITES
00699843...$9.99

FINGERPICKING BROADWAY HITS
00699838...$7.99

FINGERPICKING CELTIC FOLK
00701148...$10.99

FINGERPICKING CHILDREN'S SONGS
00699712...$9.99

FINGERPICKING CHRISTIAN
00701076...$7.99

FINGERPICKING CHRISTMAS
00699599...$9.99

FINGERPICKING CHRISTMAS CLASSICS
00701695...$7.99

FINGERPICKING CHRISTMAS SONGS
00171333...$9.99

FINGERPICKING CLASSICAL
00699620...$10.99

FINGERPICKING COUNTRY
00699687...$10.99

FINGERPICKING DISNEY
00699711...$14.99

FINGERPICKING EARLY JAZZ STANDARDS
00276565...$12.99

FINGERPICKING DUKE ELLINGTON
00699845...$9.99

FINGERPICKING ENYA
00701161...$9.99

FINGERPICKING FILM SCORE MUSIC
00160143...$12.99

FINGERPICKING GOSPEL
00701059...$9.99

FINGERPICKING GUITAR BIBLE
00691040...$19.99

FINGERPICKING HIT SONGS
00160195...$12.99

FINGERPICKING HYMNS
00699688...$9.99

FINGERPICKING IRISH SONGS
00701965...$9.99

FINGERPICKING ITALIAN SONGS
00159778...$12.99

FINGERPICKING JAZZ FAVORITES
00699844...$7.99

FINGERPICKING JAZZ STANDARDS
00699840...$10.99

FINGERPICKING ELTON JOHN
00237495...$12.99

FINGERPICKING LATIN FAVORITES
00699842...$9.99

FINGERPICKING LATIN STANDARDS
00699837...$12.99

FINGERPICKING ANDREW LLOYD WEBBER
00699839...$12.99

FINGERPICKING LOVE SONGS
00699841...$12.99

FINGERPICKING LOVE STANDARDS
00699836...$9.99

FINGERPICKING LULLABYES
00701276...$9.99

FINGERPICKING MOVIE MUSIC
00699919...$10.99

FINGERPICKING MOZART
00699794...$9.99

FINGERPICKING POP
00699615...$12.99

FINGERPICKING POPULAR HITS
00139079...$12.99

FINGERPICKING PRAISE
00699714...$10.99

FINGERPICKING ROCK
00699716...$10.99

FINGERPICKING STANDARDS
00699613...$12.99

FINGERPICKING WEDDING
00699637...$9.99

FINGERPICKING WORSHIP
00700554...$9.99

FINGERPICKING NEIL YOUNG – GREATEST HITS
00700134...$14.99

FINGERPICKING YULETIDE
00699654...$9.99

HAL•LEONARD®

Visit Hal Leonard online at **www.halleonard.com**

Prices, contents and availability subject to change without notice.